Everything You Need To Know About

SEXUAL
ABUSE

Boys and girls should be told how to protect themselves from sexual abuse.

Everything You Need To Know About
SEXUAL ABUSE

Evan Stark, Ph.D.
and
Marsha Holly, Ph.D.

THE ROSEN PUBLISHING GROUP, INC.
NEW YORK

Published in 1988, 1991, 1993, 1995, 1998 by The Rosen Publishing Group, Inc.
29 East 21st Street, New York, NY 10010

Revised Edition 1998

Copyright © 1988, 1991, 1993, 1995, 1998 by The Rosen Publishing Group, Inc.

Library of Congress Cataloging-in-Publication Data

Stark, Evan.
    Everything you need to know about sexual abuse / Evan Stark and Marsha Holly
    (The Need to know library)
    Includes bibliographical references and index.
    Summary: Identifies forms of sexual abuse and offers advice on how to get help and how to avoid such abuse.
    ISBN 0-8239-2871-3
    1. Child molesting—Juvenile literature. 2. Incest—Juvenile literature. [1. Child molesting. 2. Incest. 3. Child abuse.]
    I. Holly, Marsha II. Title. III. Series.
HQ71.S72 1995
362.7'044—dc19

                                           95-18114
                                                CIP
                                                AC

Manufactured in the United States of America

Contents

Introduction

Everyone wants to be loved. We want our parents to cherish us, and our teachers to recognize our work. We want our friends to like us. Affection and love can be expressed in many different ways.

Sometimes you may get hugs and kisses; other times you may get a pat on the back. These gestures are important and make you feel good inside. Being noticed can make you more confident and more sure of yourself. These are healthy feelings, and they remind you that you are special, in a way that nobody else is.

Maybe someone you admire is giving you extra attention, or an older friend or relative starts hanging out with you more often. This feels great, because someone recognizes how cool you are. They recognize the talents you have and make you feel important.

This attention can sometimes be confusing. When a pat on your back becomes a pat on your backside, you may be uneasy. You may question or doubt yourself. It's hard to admit that someone you trust makes you feel uncomfortable.

If someone is making you feel uncomfortable, don't be afraid to speak up. No one should touch your body without your permission. If they do, they are not showing you the respect that you deserve. When someone touches or treats you in a sexual way that makes you

Everyone likes to get attention and affection from the people that he or she loves.

feel uncomfortable, it's called sexual abuse. Sexual abuse is not an expression of love; it is hurtful. Tell someone who can help you about the abuse. Seek help from a trusted adult, either in your family, school, or community. Keep speaking up until you get the help you need to stop the abuse.

One in five girls and one in ten boys are sexually abused in some way by the time they are eighteen. Ninety percent of victims are abused by somebody they know. If you're being abused, you're not alone. Don't be embarrassed to tell. Sexual abuse is never your fault.

An invitation may not feel right. It's best to say "no."

Chapter 1

Saying No

Schchool is out for the day, and you are hanging out with your friends. A car horn honks, and you turn to see a man leaning out his car window. He looks lost.

The man calls you over to his car. He tells you he is hungry and is trying to find somewhere to eat lunch. He asks if you know of any restaurants or diners nearby.

You tell the man about a local fast-food restaurant and show him which way to go. He seems really happy and grateful. The man offers to buy you a burger if you come with him. Your stomach is growling, and lunch seems like a long time ago. Plus, the fast-food restaurant is your favorite place to eat. But your parents have always told you not to get into a stranger's car. You tell the man no thanks and go back to your friends.

Everyone has heard the familiar warning not to take candy from a stranger. If the man got out of his car, you would know to run toward your friends. If he tried to grab you, you would know to scream for help and

try to get away. You would also be sure to tell your
parents what happened so that they could report it to
the police. By telling people about this man, you may
be able to help other children and teens stay away
from him.

But what should you do when someone you know is
making you feel uncomfortable or unsafe?

*Lately you've been having some problems in math
class. You know you can do better. A few days ago, you
asked your teacher for help, and he offered to tutor
you after school. It's been helping a little bit, but you're
still not getting the hang of algebra yet.*

*During one tutoring session, you begin to feel frus-
trated and start complaining that you'll never learn
algebra. Your teacher smiles and puts his hands on
your shoulder. You think that's kind of weird, but
don't say anything. You figure that he is just trying to
be nice.*

*After a few more sessions, you find yourself know-
ing the correct answers. You feel proud of yourself,
and your teacher seems proud, too. Then he does a
strange thing. He pulls you toward him and hugs you
for a long time, rubbing your back and shoulders. You
know this doesn't feel right, but you're afraid to insult
him. After all, he spent so much time helping you.*

*When you go home, your favorite meal is on the
dinner table, but you don't feel like eating. Your mom
asks you what's wrong and you shrug because you
don't know how to explain.*

Abusers Are Often People You Trust

When you were young, you were warned about strangers who try to grab or hurt young people. Those persons are called *molesters*. Molesters are almost always men. And they are usually strangers.

But did you know that people your age are much more likely to be hurt or bothered sexually by a person they know well, such as a teacher? It could be a scout leader, a neighbor, a doctor, a coach, a minister, or the father of a friend. Or it could be a member of your own family, such as your brother, father, or stepfather. The family members who most often abuse children are fathers and brothers. However, sometimes even mothers abuse their children.

We are taught to respect and obey older persons. The hardest thing about sexual abuse is that the abuser is usually someone you trust. It may be someone who is responsible for taking care of you. It may be someone you love. It is almost always someone you want to care about you. The problem is that you may not know how to act or what to say when this happens.

The first step in dealing with sexual abuse is learning how to say no. The problem is that saying no to an adult or someone you trust is not always easy. That's why you have this book.

Teachers and parents help youngsters by listening and talking about sexual abuse.

Chapter 2

Defining Sexual Abuse

T his chapter answers questions that are often asked about sexual abuse.

What does "sexual" mean?

"Sexual" means parts of your body that can give you great pleasure when you are in love. The main sexual parts of the body are a girl's vagina and a boy's penis. These body organs are used in reproduction and are called genitals. In the story, the teacher hugged the young person in a sexual way. Touching parts of your body such as your breasts, your backside, your leg, or your mouth also can be sexual.

Sexual abuse means using a child for sexual pleasure. Sexual abuse is a crime.

Sexual abuse usually involves contact with the sexual organs of the victim's body. Many fathers kiss their children's toes, fingertips, knees, tummies, and backsides. But when those kisses or rubs are *only* on the tummy, backside, or chest—even if they aren't on the genitals—they may be bad.

The abuser may touch a young person's sexual parts or ask the child to touch his or her sexual organs. Or the abuser may use the young person in some other sexual activity.

A male may put his penis into a girl's vagina. This is called *intercourse*. A female abuser may force a young boy to have intercourse. When a child has intercourse with a parent, brother, or sister, this is called *incest*. Pregnancy and venereal diseases are some of the dangerous results when the abuse includes intercourse. When a man puts his penis in a child's anus, it is *sodomy*. Sexual abuse may be very painful, and it leaves deep emotional scars.

Who are the victims of sexual abuse?

Girls are more likely to be abused than boys. However, boys can be abused as well. Whether the victim is a boy or a girl, most cases of sexual abuse are committed by men. But that is not always true because women can also commit sexual abuse.

Children are at the greatest risk of being sexually abused between the ages of nine and twelve years. But a child of two or a young adult of 17 can also become a victim of sexual abuse.

Have many people been sexually abused?

Sexual abuse is far more common than most people think. So is incest.

Count the girls and boys in your class. Do you think any kids in your class had an experience like the kid in the story? Some may have. One out of every five girls and one out of every ten boys may be sexually abused before they reach eighteen.

Are all sexual abusers violent?

Many sexual abusers use physical force. Others use threats. The abuser may threaten to harm someone the child loves, such as her mother or the family pet. Or a parent may say he will leave forever if the child tells their secret. He may even claim that a policeman will take the child away. As a result, the child may start to fear the very people who can rescue her from the abuse.

However, sexual abuse doesn't always involve force or threats. Many abusers use bribes or presents to convince the child to do what they want. Money, a new video game, or a trip to the zoo or the park can be tempting.

Often sexual abuse begins as a game, such as tickling or play-wrestling. The abuser wants the child to trust him. After he gains the child's trust, the game becomes sexual.

Does sexual abuse always hurt?

Sexual abuse can cause serious problems even when there is no violence or intercourse. Children who are abused feel isolated from other children. They may feel ashamed about what has happened. They may think they are not worth much. Those feelings are called low self-esteem. They may feel so angry that they hurt another child, or a pet. Or they may try to hurt themselves. Some children who are sexually abused become very sad or withdrawn. This is called depression.

Sexual abuse can also cause problems when a child becomes an adult. Adults who were sexually abused often don't trust others. Or they may want to avoid sex altogether.

The longer sexual abuse goes on, the more damage it can cause.

Not all children who are sexually abused suffer long-term effects. If the abuse is stopped early and the child finds someone they trust to talk to, many of the harmful effects of sexual abuse can be prevented.

Who commits sexual abuse?

A myth is something most people believe that is not true. One myth is that sexual abusers are sick. Another myth is that sexual abuse only happens in families that have a lot of other problems as well.

Some abusers have serious mental health problems. Some are sexually attracted to children, but not to other adults. And some abusers were sexually or physically abused themselves when they were children. Some families where sexual abuse

Finding a friend to talk to can help stop abuse.

occurs also have other problems. The husband may be beating his wife. The mother may be disabled.

But most sexual abuse occurs in ordinary families and is committed by ordinary men.

The abuser wants things his own way. He likes being in control and having power over others. This is why he is attracted to someone who is smaller and weaker than he is, like a child.

How have we learned so much about sexual abuse?

We learn about sexual abuse when people who have been sexually abused tell their stories.

Adults who were hurt by sexual abuse as children are talking about it. Children are talking too. They are telling their stories to teachers, nurses, parents, and friends—to anyone who will listen.

Parents, doctors, teachers, police, and others who want to help and protect children are learning about sexual abuse.

Sexual abuse is on TV and the radio and in the newspapers. Young people all over are speaking out. Sexual abuse is the secret that is now being shared.

Chapter 3

Rules to Remember About Sexual Abuse

The stories in this book come from girls and boys who got help. The boys and girls use seven rules to solve their problems. These rules can help you understand and respond to sexual abuse.

Rule #1. YOUR BODY BELONGS TO YOU.

You, and only you, should decide how to use your body sexually. In sexual abuse, someone who is older and more powerful decides how to use your body. This is wrong. You have a right to say no.

Rule #2. SEXUAL ABUSE IS NEVER YOUR FAULT.

Children are not responsible for what adults or other older persons do. Abuse is not their fault, even if they cannot say no or if they enjoy the attention they get from the abuser. Nothing a child does, or doesn't do, excuses an older person who uses a child for sexual pleasure.

Some men attend counseling sessions to discuss their problems
as abusers.

Rule #3. <u>SEXUAL ABUSE IS ALWAYS</u>
   <u>HARMFUL</u>.

Sexual abuse always hurts the child. Sometimes
the child's body is hurt. If a girl who is old enough
to have babies is abused, she can get pregnant. But
the deepest hurt is the way sexual abuse makes
children feel. Sexual abuse always makes children
feel bad about themselves. These feelings can make
it hard to work in school, to have friends, or to
have fun.

Rule #4. <u>GOOD PEOPLE CAN DO BAD</u>
   <u>THINGS</u>.

It is hard to believe that someone we love or who
is kind to us can sexually abuse us. Abusers may
be good persons in other ways. They may give
presents. Or they may be gentle when they want
sex. But the abuse is very, very wrong and must be
stopped.

Rule #5. <u>SEXUAL ABUSE DOES NOT STOP</u>
   <u>BY ITSELF</u>.

Sexual abuse is hard to talk about. Children are
sometimes afraid of the abuser. But sexual abuse
usually goes on until the abuser is made to stop.
The best way to stop sexual abuse is to tell an adult
who will listen and do something about it.

There are special people, child workers, whose
job is to protect children from abuse. Adults know
how to find these people.

Sexual abuse always hurts. It creates feelings of shame and loneliness.

Rule #6. KEEP TELLING PEOPLE YOU TRUST ABOUT SEXUAL ABUSE UNTIL SOMEONE LISTENS.

Some adults may not believe a child. Other adults may tell the young person to forget about the problem. But remember, sexual abuse does not stop by itself. If one adult doesn't do the right thing, tell another who will.

Rule #7. WHAT HAPPENS TO A SEXUAL ABUSER IS NEVER YOUR FAULT.

Children feel, "If I tell, then what happens to the abuser is my fault." Because sexual abuse is a crime, some abusers go to jail. Others leave the house. When the abuser is someone you care about, this is very hard. Some abusers stop when they are told it is wrong. Some abusers need to see a doctor. Remember, only the sexual abuser is responsible for what happens when abuse is uncovered.

The next few chapters tell the stories of children who said no to abuse. See if the Seven Rules help you understand what happened to them—and what they did *to help themselves*.

Chapter 4

Good People Can Do Bad Things

Debra lives in a house with her mom, her dad, her grandfather and her dog. After her eleventh birthday party, she looked at herself in the mirror. She noticed that her breasts were beginning to form.

Sexual Abusers Can Be Family Members

Suddenly, Debra's grandfather walked into the room. He laughed at her in front of the mirror. He made fun of her body.

"I suppose you think you need a bra," he teased.

Debra felt hurt. She had wondered if she could wear a bra. Some of her friends wore them already. But what her grandfather said made her feel ashamed. When he made fun of her, she thought she was no good.

A few weeks later, her grandfather walked into the bathroom while Debra was taking a bath. At first

25

A father should respect his daughter's privacy.

she thought it was a mistake. But he wouldn't leave when she asked him. She wrapped a towel around herself. But he yanked it off. Then he grabbed her from behind. He held her breasts.

"Cut it out," she yelled. She tried to get free.

"You used to like being tickled," he said.

"I'm not a little girl anymore," Debra said. She got really angry. She felt dirty and wanted to die. He told her not to tell her parents or he would have to leave the house.

She didn't want her grandfather to go. Although he kept bothering her, she decided not to tell her mom and dad.

Debra is growing up. Her body is changing. She feels bashful because she is not always sure what's happening. She needs time to get used to her body. It's really a new body all the time. Debra needs privacy to explore herself and learn about her body. She has a right to privacy. Some day she will want someone her own age to touch her breasts. And that's okay.

Her grandfather has no respect for Debra. He wants to see her naked. He pretends he's kidding. But abuse is no joke.

Tell Someone You Trust

One day, Mrs. Markle, a teacher at Debra's school, saw her crying in the girl's bathroom. Debra told Mrs. Markle why she was so upset. Mrs. Markle questioned Debra closely. Then she told

Debra she had done the right thing to tell her. She explained that there was no reason for Debra to hate herself. The feelings she has about herself come from her grandfather's abuse.

Mrs. Markle called a social worker at the child protection office and the social worker came to the house. She explained that Debra's grandpa would have to live somewhere else.

When Debra got home, her mother was angry. "Why didn't you just tell me what happened?" she yelled.

"I didn't think you would believe me," Debra said. "And grandpa told me not to tell or he would have to leave the house."

"I don't want grandpa to go either but he'll have to." her mother said. "I'm really upset you didn't tell me. I would have stopped him."

Remembering the Rules

The most important lesson Debra learned was Rule #1, Your Body Belongs to You.

It's *your* body. You have a right to have your body respected, comforted, and loved only in ways that please you or that benefit you.

Rule #2, Abuse Is Never Your Fault.

Nothing Debra did was wrong. Children are not responsible for the sexual behavior of adults.

Rule #4, Good People Do Bad Things.

Debra's grandfather may be good in other ways. But his abuse is wrong and must be stopped.

Finding someone who will listen is the first step toward ending abuse.

Community Leaders Can Be Abusers

Debra's abuser was a family member. Chris and Ronnie were sexually abused by one of the most respected people in town—the Catholic priest. Chris' abuse started when he was 17; Ronnie was 13. Both came from homes without fathers. They needed the love and respect of an older man, someone who would be like a father to them. The priest took advantage of that need.

Ronnie is older now, but he is deeply troubled by his past. He has had serious thoughts of suicide.

Chris and Ronnie didn't know each other. For a long time, neither said anything to anyone. They were afraid of what might happen to themselves and to the priest. Both wanted to believe that this man did love them. They didn't want to admit they were being abused.

It's hard to believe that people we love and respect can treat us cruelly. But it does happen sometimes. Even people who are well-known and loved by your community—religious leaders, counselors, politicians, and school administrators— can betray a trust and become abusers. When and if that occurs, we must admit what is happening and get help right away.

This does not mean that you should become suspicious of all adults. Most people are good. It means that you should recognize sexual abuse when you see or hear about it. Keep in mind Rule #4, Good People Can Do Bad Things.

Chapter 5

Sexual Abuse Is Never Your Fault

Leota is almost nine. She lives with her mother and her seventeen-year-old brother, Alonzo. They live in a two-room apartment. She and Alonzo share a room. Sometimes her mother works at night. When this happens, Alonzo baby-sits. When Leota goes to bed, Alonzo stays up to watch TV.

Leota's friends think Alonzo is a great dancer. Leota wishes Alonzo would pay attention to her. When she tries to get his attention, he tells her to shut up or go away.

Leota's Brother Is an Abuser

The first time Alonzo bothered Leota in bed, she was almost asleep. She felt hands on her bottom. She thought it was her mother tucking her in. The next night she heard Alonzo cross the room. He sat

Sexual abuse can destroy the trust between a brother and sister.

on the edge of her bed. He put his hand in her pajamas. He felt around below her tummy. Then he went back to his bed. She lay awake and felt scared.

A week later her brother touched her again. This time she pretended to be asleep. He put his hand in her pajamas and started rubbing her genitals. When this happened she had a tingling feeling. She was also confused. She wanted Alonzo to like her. She knew that what he was doing was wrong. But she thought it was her fault.

Alonzo continued to sexually abuse Leota. When Alonzo rubbed her, neither of them spoke. Several times he even got under the covers with Leota. Then he rubbed his penis against her. She kept her eyes closed. Outside the bedroom Alonzo pretended Leota didn't exist.

Leota started to worry all the time. She felt different from her friends. She stayed by herself. She was sure everyone knew about her and Alonzo. She had trouble in school. She failed tests in spelling, her best subject.

One day Maria, a girl in Leota's class, asked what was wrong. Leota told her. Maria listened

Leota started to worry all the time. She felt different from her friends. She stayed by herself.

carefully. She didn't fully understand. But she knew Alonzo was hurting Leota. The next day Maria's mother called Leota's mother on the phone. They talked for a long time.

That night Leota's mother stayed home from work. She made Alonzo move his bed into the living room. She moved her own bed into the room with Leota. The next time she had to work at night she called Carmen, Maria's older sister, to baby-sit for Leota.

Leota's mother called a child worker. The child worker made Alonzo go to a doctor about his problem.

For several weeks Leota blushed whenever she saw Alonzo. Then she felt okay. She and Maria became best friends.

A year later, Alonzo told Leota he was sorry about what he had done.

Remembering the Rules

The most important lesson Leota learned was Rule #2, Sexual Abuse Is Never Your Fault.

Leota knew that Alonzo liked to touch her. She loved her brother. She wanted him to hug her and love her back. She thought he would love her more if she let him do what he wanted.

Children want and need affection. Sometimes older people make it hard to get affection in good

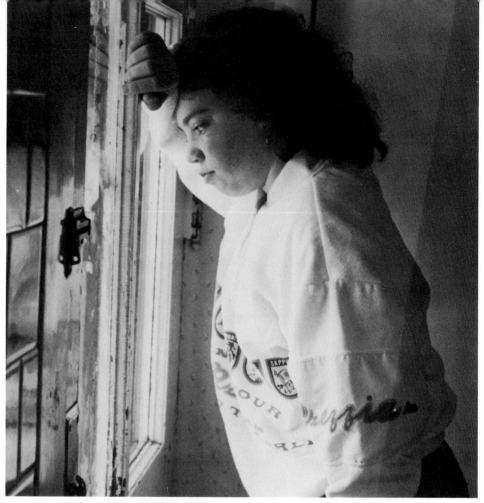
Constant worrying may lead to depression.

ways. Children sometimes think they have to get it any way they can. But no matter how a child acts, she or he should not be abused.

Leota lay in her bed quietly when Alonzo touched her. Does that mean what happened was her fault? No. The victim of sexual abuse is never to blame. Children simply are not responsible for what an older, stronger person does.

Rule #5 is Sexual Abuse Does Not Stop by Itself.

Maria saw something was wrong. She asked to help. This was very brave. But Maria could not stop Alonzo. So she told her mother. When Alonzo's mother found out, she called a child worker. A child worker's job is to protect children from abuse. Alonzo would not have stopped bothering his sister if Maria had not told her mother.

Rule #7 is What Happens to the Abuser Is Never Your Fault.

Alonzo's bed was moved. He had to go for help. All this was his fault, not Leota's. Still, Leota felt sorry for Alonzo.

The Oprah Winfrey Story

Many famous people have suffered sexual abuse. Talk-show host Oprah Winfrey is one of them. When she was 9, she was raped by her 19-year-old cousin. From then until she was 14, she was sexually abused by a friend of the family. A favorite uncle also molested her. "You lose your childhood when you've been abused," says Oprah.

At last, when she was 14, Oprah went to live with her father, Vernon. Only then did the abuse stop. But a great deal of damage had already been done. For years the famous TV star lived a tortured life because of her past. She felt guilty and ashamed. It took Oprah a long time to realize Rule #2 about sexual abuse: Sexual Abuse Is Never

Sometimes older people make it hard to get affection in good ways.

Your Fault. "The truth is, the child is never to blame," Oprah now believes. "It took me 37 years to figure that out."

One night Oprah heard a news report that a four-year-old Chicago girl had been abused, strangled, and thrown into a lake. "I vowed that night to do something, to take a stand for the children of this country," she said. Today Oprah Winfrey is using her popularity and her television show to help other young victims of sexual abuse.

Oprah suggested an idea for a new law. The law would require that a list be kept of all people convicted of child abuse and similar crimes. When a person applied for a job working with children, such as at a school, day care center, or camp, the person's name would be checked against this list. Some states have this law, but Oprah wants all states to have it.

"We have to [show] that we value our children," she believes. So she's also working on a plan to have the law punish every child molester. "These people must know," she says, "that when you hurt a child, this is what happens to you."

Oprah Winfrey learned Rule #5 the hard way: Sexual Abuse Does Not Stop By Itself. She knows that in order to make it stop, people must take action.

Abused children sometimes become bullies.

Chapter 6

Boys Are Victims, Too

Billy was eleven years old. A seven-year-old boy named Sam lived next door. Sam had a rabbit named Black Jack. Sam loved Black Jack very much.

One day the boys were alone in Billy's yard. Billy told Sam to follow him into the garage. "I have something special for you," Billy said. Billy closed the door. He unzipped his pants and took out his penis. He grabbed Sam by the neck and pushed him down.

"Put it in your mouth," he told Sam. "If you don't, I'll kill Black Jack." Sam did what Billy said.

Billy told Sam his father and mother would die if he told. "And I won't be your friend," Billy said. Sam was very scared. So he kept the secret.

Sam was in the first grade. At school he started hitting other children. The teacher asked Sam's parents if anything was wrong. She also asked Sam. But he kept quiet.

Things got worse. Sam started to wet his bed. He woke up in the night crying. His mother went to his bed. Sam said, "I don't want you to die, Mommy."

One day Sam was in the bathroom at school with another little boy. They had their pants down. Sam grabbed the boy. He pointed to his penis. "Take it in your mouth," he said. The boy knocked Sam down, and Sam cried. Then Sam told the teacher what Billy had made him do in the garage. The teacher was very upset. She told Sam's parents. She also called a child worker.

Sam's father yelled at Billy. Later he yelled at Billy's mother. Billy started to cry. He told his mother that a bigger boy had been making him do the same thing he made Sam do. The bigger boy was a bully. Billy was afraid of him, just as Sam was afraid of Billy.

The child worker went to Sam's house. First she talked to Sam, then to Billy. She also visited the bully and his family. The bully was sent for help.

Remembering the Rules

The most important lesson to learn from this story is Rule #3, Sexual Abuse Is Always Harmful.

Sometimes children who are sexually abused will abuse other children who are weaker. Or they may hurt pets. When Billy was abused, he didn't know what to do. He was scared. But he was also angry. He felt that this should not have happened to a big boy like him. Maybe something was wrong with him, he thought. He felt bad about himself. He didn't want anyone to find out that he was weak. So he proved he was stronger than Sam. He abused his friend.

When a Boy Is Sexually Abused

In our society, boys and men are expected to be tough. If you cry, people may say you're a sissy. If you can't protect yourself, people may say you're a wimp. Of course this thinking is silly. But it's one reason why most cases of sexual abuse never get reported when males are the victims.

The truth is that one out of every ten boys will probably suffer some kind of sexual abuse before he is eighteen. Many times the victims are boys who have no fathers at home or whose fathers show no love for them. The abuser is often someone the boy knows, a family friend or relative.

Some boys are afraid that being abused by a man makes them *homosexual.* A homosexual is a person who has sexual feelings toward people of the same sex. This keeps many male victims silent about the abuse. But, boys as well as girls, remember, if you have been sexually abused, speak up!

Two sisters share the hurt of their father's sexual abuse.

Chapter 7

Incest and Rape

Selina is 11 years old and lives with her parents. Selina's mother works late sometimes, so she is alone with her father a lot. Lately, he has been getting into her bed at night. He takes off her underpants and touches her and sometimes he forces Selina to touch him too. Selina doesn't like what her father is doing, but she's afraid to tell her mother.

Sexual abuse is always devastating. The victims of sexual abuse often feel isolated, confused, and distrustful of others. There are many different types of sexual abuse. This chapter considers incest and rape.

What Is Incest?

Incest is any sexual activity between people who are closely related to each other. Someone who is closely related to you can be a family member who lives in your house, like your father or your sister or your stepfather or stepsister. Or it can be a relative who does not live with you, like your uncle or your grandfather.

Any sexual activity between a child and another

family member can be called incest. Incest is not limited to the act of sexual intercourse. If a member of your family touches private parts of your body, that is considered incest. If a family member makes you look at or touch parts of his or her naked body, that is incest. When a family member forces you to watch or be a part of *pornographic* pictures, or pictures that involve sexual acts, that is incest, too.

Who Commits Incest?

Incest happens in all types of homes. It can happen in families that are rich and in families that are underprivileged. It can happen in homes where parents are living together or in homes where parents are divorced or separated. Although the abuser is often male—a father, a brother, an uncle, a grandfather—that is not always the case. Sometimes the abuser is a female family member. The type of incest that is most difficult for a child to recover from is that committed by a parent. Children trust their parents to protect them from harm. When a parent sexually abuses a child, that trust is shattered.

Incest most often occurs in homes where the abuser was a victim of incest as a child. Incestuous families may prefer to keep to themselves. They don't want their behavior, which they know is wrong, to be discovered by others.

Many abusers have trouble getting along with people their own age. They have few friends. They may try to keep their victims from having friends to prevent them from telling someone about the abuse.

When an abuser is discovered, he or she may not accept responsibility for his or her actions. He or she may make excuses or try to blame someone else. For instance, a father might try to justify his incestuous actions by saying that it is better for him to have sex with his daughter than with a woman outside of the family. An older cousin might say that she and her younger cousin were just "playing doctor." A lonely mother might approach her oldest son for sex if her husband is dead. But the truth of the matter is that incest can *never* be justified. It is always wrong. The abuser is to blame.

Victims of Incest

Incest is among the worst forms of sexual abuse. It destroys a family's trust in one another. Victims of incest are often angry with their abuser because they once trusted that person. Incest victims may also be angry with other members of the family for failing to protect them. Sometimes family members fail to recognize the warning signs of sexual abuse within the family. Sometimes they refuse to acknowledge the abuse even when they are told about it. It can be very hard, even for adults, to believe that someone in their family could commit such a horrible act. Find someone who will listen. If you think you may be the victim of incest, tell someone—a school counselor, a teacher, a friend's parent—what is going on. Keep talking until someone takes action to stop the abuse.

What Is Rape and Who Commits It?

Rape is the crime of forcing a person to have sexual intercourse against his or her will. This means the forced act of putting a penis in someone's mouth, anus, or vagina. We tend to think of rape as a man forcing a female to have sex, but men and boys can also be raped.

Rape, like all acts of sexual abuse, is most frequently committed by someone the victim knows. The rapist may be a member of the victim's family, a family friend, or a community leader such as a teacher, coach, or church official. Both men and women commit rape. Rapists are most often adults. However, other children or young adults can also be guilty of rape.

Many rapists were sexually abused themselves. People who rape children are known as *pedophiles*. Boys are usually raped by men. These pedophiles are usually *heterosexual* (having sexual feelings toward people of the opposite sex). When they have sex with someone their own age, they prefer women. When they rape a child, however, they do not always choose a victim of the opposite sex. Sometimes, they choose a victim of the same sex.

Megan Kanka was a 7-year-old girl who lived in New Jersey. No one in her neighborhood was aware that the man who lived across the street from her home was a twice-convicted sexual offender. He sexually abused and killed Megan.

Her murder prompted New Jersey lawmakers to pass a package of laws, known commonly as Megan's Law, which deal with sex offenders after they have been released from prison. One of these laws requires the police to notify the neighborhood, nearby schools, and other institutions when a convicted sex offender is moving into the area. This shows the importance of the issue of sexual abuse of children and teens.

The Aftermath of Rape

Like all forms of sexual abuse, rape can cause long-lasting emotional problems for the victim. Rape victims often battle for years with shame, guilt, depression, and anxiety. This is discussed further in Chapter 8.

Rape can also cause physical injury and enduring health problems. Delicate body tissues can be torn or damaged during rape. George was six years old when he was first raped by his cousin. "He pulled my pajama bottoms down and forced his penis into my anus. The skin broke and I began to bleed." Rape victims often bleed or are literally scarred as a result of being raped.

Another health concern for a rape victim is venereal disease. A rapist who has a sexually transmitted disease (STD) can pass this disease on to his or her victim. AIDS is the most dangerous STD; there is no cure for it. Other STDs such as gonorrhea and syphilis can cause permanent damage if they are not treated medically. They can be life-threatening if left untreated.

Pregnancy can also result from rape if the victim is a girl or a woman of childbearing age. Because of all the possible health complications that can result from rape, it is extremely important for a victim to seek medical attention immediately. A victim of rape should go directly to an emergency room without showering, changing clothes, or cleaning up. A thorough medical examination will protect the victim's health. It can also provide physical evidence of rape that can be used in bringing the rapist to justice.

Each year, thousands of cases of sexual abuse, including rape and incest, go unreported. If you have been abused by someone you know and care about, it may seem difficult to report the crime to the police. Many children worry that if they report incest they will be taken from their home. Others fear that the abuser will be sent away, or even sent to prison. But sexual abuse is a crime. What Happens To A Sexual Abuser Is Never Your Fault. Sexual abusers must be forced to stop their pattern of abuse or they will continue to abuse you. They may also be abusing other people. When you report a case of sexual abuse, you help protect yourself and other potential victims. There are programs designed to help sexual abusers stop their destructive crimes. Remember, even if the abuser is your mother or father, Keep Talking Until Someone Listens.

Chapter 8

Help for Sexual Abuse Victims

Sexual abuse hurts victims physically and emotionally. A number of programs are specially designed to help victims cope. If you have been sexually abused in the past or if you are currently being abused, it will be extremely helpful if you find and participate in one of these programs. Depending upon the circumstances of your abuse, you may wish to participate in a program that is designed to support you alone. Or you may choose a program that will offer support to you and other members of your family.

A parent who listens and tries to understand helps heal a victim of sexual abuse.

Whatever type of program you choose to meet your emotional needs, it is also important that your physical needs are addressed.

Medical Care

If you have been sexually abused, your body has been violated. It is only natural to wonder whether your body has suffered any long-lasting damage. See a doctor, especially if you experienced any pain, bruising, or bleeding as a result of abuse. A medical examination will determine whether your body has been injured in any way. The doctor will look for signs of injury including bruises and scar tissue. The doctor may also test for pregnancy and STDs.

Probably you will need to visit your doctor's office only once. However, if you are pregnant or have contracted an STD, you will need to see the doctor again.

Counseling

Victims of sexual abuse must cope with a number of confusing emotions. Even if you are no longer being abused, you may feel anger, hostility, and shame, and you may feel as if you have little control of your own body. In fact, someone *has* used your body without your permission. You may experience periods of anxiety or depression. It will take time for you to heal. But you will heal.

Some effects of sexual abuse can continue into adulthood if you don't seek out help. The love and support of caring family members and friends can help ease your mind during the rough times to come. Still, it is best to talk with someone who understands the emotions that sexual abuse victims feel. You may want to find other survivors of sexual abuse with whom you can share your feelings. If this is the case, you may wish to speak with a therapist.

Finding a Therapist

A therapist is a professional who is trained to listen and to help people sort through their emotions. It is possible to find a therapist who works primarily with victims of sexual abuse. A therapist can be an employee of a mental health agency or a protective service agency. You can ask your school counselor or another adult to help you locate a therapist.

If that idea makes you uncomfortable, you can find a therapist on your own. If you have reported your sexual abuse to a human services agency, you can call that same agency again. They should have a list of experienced sexual abuse therapists in your area. Even if you have not reported your case, a human services agency is a good place to begin your search. Your local telephone book will have a listing of Human Services or Social Services agencies you can call.

People who sexually abuse children were often abused as children.

Your medical doctor may also be able to put you in contact with a sexual abuse therapist. Do not hesitate to call your doctor or a local hospital for a referral.

The next step is to make an appointment to see one of the therapists to whom you have been referred. The therapist is there to help you. A good therapist will not attempt to force you to talk about anything that makes you uncomfortable. For the most part, he or she will do a lot of listening.

You may feel comfortable right away talking to the therapist. If so, you are on your way. However, if you do not feel comfortable right away, don't be alarmed. This is a new experience, and it may take a few appointments for you to feel at ease. If you still feel uncomfortable after several visits, don't give up! It may be that the therapist is simply not the right one for you. Make an appointment to speak with another therapist. Chances are you will feel more comfortable talking with him or her.

Individual Counseling

Individual counseling gives you the chance to share your feelings about sexual abuse and its effects on you in a private atmosphere. Only you and the therapist are present.

The therapist will not judge you. He or she knows that you are not to blame for the abuse. There is no need for you to feel any pressure to discuss aspects of the abuse that you are not yet ready to talk about. The therapist knows from experience with other victims that talking about abuse can be difficult and painful. Some victims may feel uncomfortable talking about the abuse for weeks or even months. If you are not ready to talk about the abuse or your feelings concerning it, your therapist may use other methods to try and help you, or he or she may ask you what you would like to discuss.

Some victims of sexual abuse prefer to write about their feelings in a journal and then allow their therapist to read the journal. Others may want to draw a picture or make a painting to express themselves. Children, in particular, often use dolls or puppets to show their therapist what type of abuse they suffered. A therapist should allow you to express yourself in whatever way you find the most comfortable.

The amount of time needed for counseling is unique to each person. Someone who was abused once is likely to need less counseling than someone who suffered repeated abuse over a long period.

Group Counseling

Many sexual abuse victims feel isolated from their peers. They have suffered abuse that makes them feel different from their friends. A victim may feel as though he or she is the only person who has suffered in this way. Victims who have these feelings may benefit from group counseling. Group counseling consists of a small number of victims and a counselor who leads the group's discussions. Many groups are made up of members of approximately the same age.

Group counseling gives a victim the opportunity to meet and talk with others who have experienced similar abuse. Group members realize that they are not alone, that there are other people who

Through therapy, survivors of sexual abuse can come to trust other people again.

share similar experiences and feelings. They learn from each other. They learn how to cope with and express their feelings in a healthy way. They learn how to deal with family members and friends. Group members learn that they can depend on the support given to one another as each of them faces new emotional challenges relating to the abuse. By learning to depend on each other, victims begin to trust other people again, which is an important step in the healing process.

Most sexual abuse victims undergo some individual counseling before they feel ready to join a group. Many people, as well as many therapists, feel it is helpful for victims to continue with individual counseling, but participate in group counseling as well. It is up to you and the therapist to decide what type of counseling or combination of counseling is best for you. Your therapist will not make a decision without getting your approval first.

Other Counseling Scenarios

Many sexual abuse victims feel anger toward their parents. It is a parent's role to protect his or her child from harm. Abuse victims may feel let down by the failure of their parents or one of their parents to protect them. If this is the case, you may benefit from counseling with one or both of your parents. It is likely that you and your parents have issues that you would like to discuss regarding your relationship. It may prove helpful to discuss these matters under the guidance of a therapist. A good therapist will help you redirect your anger in other directions so that it will not harm you or anyone else. If your family is to function in a healthy manner, it is essential that your faith in your parent or parents be restored.

Perhaps you have been sexually abused by one of your parents. If this is the case, you may wish to participate in ongoing counseling with your abusive parent. But such counseling sessions should never be forced on you. You should have the right to decide when you feel ready to confront your abusive parent or if you wish to confront him or her at all. When your parent abused you, he or she wrongly assumed control of your body. Now you have the opportunity to be in control instead of your parent.

Chapter 9

Cruising the Information Superhighway

Computers are everywhere, from cash registers to cars to airplanes. You probably have used one yourself, perhaps in an arcade, classroom, or library.

If you've used a computer, you've probably been on the Internet, too. It is sometimes referred to as the information superhighway or the World Wide Web because it contains so much information. The Internet can be a great place to learn new things or talk to people.

The Internet has places that people can visit on their computers to discuss their interests with others. These are called chatrooms. Chatrooms can seem like a great way to make new friends but, just as you know you shouldn't get into a stranger's car on the street, you should use caution when having conversations on your computer with strangers. You can see the stranger in the car; in a chatroom, all you know about this stranger is whatever he chooses to tell you. And what he tells you may not be true.

Some sexual abusers are using the Internet to find victims. They usually use a chatroom to make friends with a young person, often by pretending to be a child or teen themselves. They convince their victim to meet with them personally and then sexually abuse him or her. The Federal Bureau of Investigation (FBI) has several suggestions for preventing sexual abuse for kids and teens who use the Internet.

- First, never give out identifying information such as your name, address, phone number, or photograph to anyone without first getting your parent's permission;
- Never respond to messages that are obscene, suggestive, threatening, or that make you feel uncomfortable in any way;
- Always tell your parents if someone makes you feel uncomfortable;
- Never arrange a face-to-face meeting with anyone you meet on the Internet unless you have your parents join you and meet in a public place.

The world can seem like a scary place, especially if you have been sexually abused. If somebody is abusing you or someone you know, remember the rules and tell someone immediately. You can cope, recover, heal, and live a healthy, happy life. Take the first step— speak up.

Glossary

abuser Someone who tries to hurt you sexually.

genitals These are sexual organs. Examples of genitals are a boy's penis and a girl's vagina.

heterosexual Having sexual feelings toward people of the opposite sex.

homosexual Having sexual feelings toward people of the same sex.

incest Sexual activity between two people who are closely related.

intercourse When a male's penis is placed inside the vagina of a female.

molester A stranger or someone you barely know who tries to hurt you sexually.

pedophile An adult who enjoys sexual activity with children.

pornography Pictures, films, or stories that clearly show sexual activity for the purpose of arousing sexual desire.

privacy The right to be left alone.

psychologist A doctor who studies the mind and helps treat mental problems.

rape When one person forces another person to have sexual relations.

survivor Someone who was hurt or abused in the past.

therapist A person trained to help treat mental or physical problems.

victim Someone who is being hurt or abused.

Where to Go for Help

There are many places you can go that can help you stop sexual abuse. Teachers, social workers, doctors, counselors, religious leaders, and police officers can help you. If you can't find assistance or want information on helping someone who is being sexually abused, call one of the numbers below:

Childhelp USA
(800) 4-A-CHILD
This hotline is open 24 hours-a-day.

The National Clearinghouse on Child Abuse and Neglect Information
(800) 394-3366
This is not a direct hotline, but a place where you can get written information.
Web site: http://www.calib.com/nccanch

National Committee for Prevention of Child Abuse
(800) CHILDREN
They will help you find a chapter in your state.

For Further Reading

Bean, Barbara, and Shari Bennett. *The Me Nobody Knows: A Guide for Teen Survivors.* New York: Jossey-Bass Publishers, 1998.

Gillham, Bill. *The Facts About Child Sexual Abuse.* New York: Cassell Academic, 1991.

Hyde, Margaret O., and Elizabeth Held Forsyth. *The Sexual Abuse of Children and Adolescents: From Infants to Adolescents.* Brookfield, CT: Millbrook Press, 1997.

Reinert, Dale Robert. *Sexual Abuse and Incest.* Springfield, NJ: Enslow Publishers, 1998.

Reynolds, Marilyn. *Telling.* Buena Park, CA: Morning Glory Press, 1996.

Terkel, Susan Neiburg. *Finding Your Way: A Book About Sexual Ethics.* Danbury, CT: Franklin Watts, 1996.

Watts, C. Ellen. *It Can't Happen to Me.* Cincinnati, OH: Standard Publishing, 1990.

Wooden, Kenneth. *Child Lures: What Every Parent and Child Should Know About Preventing Sexual Abuse and Abduction.* Arlington, TX: Summit Publishing Group, 1995.

Index

About the Author

Evan Stark is a well-known sociologist, educator, and therapist as well as a popular lecturer on women's and children's health issues. Dr. Stark was the Henry Rutgers Fellow at Rutgers University, an associate at the Institution for Social and Policy Studies at Yale University, and a Fulbright Fellow at the University of Essex. He is the author of many publications in the field of family relations and is the father of four children.

Acknowledgments and Photo Credits

Cover photo by Stuart Rabinowitz; p. 20 by Blackbirch Graphics, Inc.; all other photos by Stuart Rabinowitz.